Tennessee Boy

To: Jim & Gloria

Tennessee Boy

Life Sketches and Poems

Peace & Blessings forever!
Fondly,
Robert W. Cole

by

Robert W. Cole

ZION PUBLISHING

Cover art by Michael Brown

Library of Congress Control Number: 2016953455

1. Tennessee Boy 2. Autobiography

3. Poetry

ISBN 978-0-9627147-8-8

ZION PUBLISHING

1500 Crown Colony Ct. #540

Des Moines, Iowa 50315

Printed in the United States of America

≈ My Mantra ≈

To know who you are

is to know what you are about.

That gives us time to expose

our mind, heart and soul

to define the spirit and purpose for living.

≈ Robert W. Cole

"I extend myself to others through my compassionate thoughts and actions. Throughout the day I behold the Christ in others and send them compassion-filled thoughts and prayers. These heart to heart connections enhance any sense of oneness in the world. We are one with God and one with each other."

≈ *Anonymous*

≈ DEDICATION ≈

I am thankful to have good friends, surrogate sons and family checking to see about my welfare daily and weekly. Without the support of these caring people, where would I be today?

You have made my life richer and more bountiful than I could have ever imagined.

Thank you.

≈ Remembrances ≈

In loving memory of my Mother

Beatrice Banks Cole

and my Aunt

Pearl Banks Elliot

and the inspiration gained from

Mrs. Ella B. Couch

for sharing the wit and wisdom

of her 106 years of living

≈ Acknowledgments ≈

Special thanks to:

Michael Hairston

For his encouragement and dedication as we traveled on this journey together and

Michael Brown

For transforming my life journey into a thoughtful and imaginative design for the cover of this book.

Delores Brisbon
Melvin and Julia Gauthia
Robert Howard
Michael Mann
Mark and Maria Rocktashel
Tracy and Minerva Smith
Darnel and Brenda Thomas

For their wisdom and insight into life's challenges and how to survive the many changes one will make in a lifetime.

≈ FOREWORD ≈

The Earth turns on its axis and once a year it circles the Sun. The longer you live, the seasons' cycles appear to come and go with increasing speed, but the motion never wanes or waxes like the moon. Time never stops. Rare celestial occurrences come and go, and the wise hold fast to scriptural warnings of signs of the End of Days. Believe what you wish, but never forget cause and effect and the revolutions around the Sun bring understanding through cycles of time.

Technology has its firm grip on daily life. Facts crawl, news breaks, sound bytes by bits, and 140 characters are the length of intelligence-speak among circles of friends, but thank God for poetic insight and this second collection of wisdom and witticisms by Bob Cole. Like the perpetual turning of this planet, his words are constant as the "old school" analog clock he winds to keep pace with a world spinning out of control. The chimes from the mechanics of his well-tuned timepiece and the art of writing keep his life in balance to share what he has learned.

This biographical sketch and collection of poetry is a call to any reader running wild to the flashing numerals of the digital clock. Poetry takes time for reading and reflection, and even if you never learned to respect the wisdom of the elders, it's never too late to learn. Make time for relaxation with this book.

This sage advice will bring a century of thoughtful reflection, and while it may not be the blueprint for success, it is food for thought, to teach you what not to do as the Earth turns in your lifetime.

Ty Collins

≈ Tennessee Boy Timeline ≈

	1948	My Father, William Bonaparte Cole, died
Graduated From Tennessee State University with Bachelor of Music Degree with major in organ music	*1952*	
Taught music K-12 in Itta Bena, Mississippi for three months	*1953*	
Served in the US Army as Chaplain's assistant stationed in Korea with travels to Japan		
Studied organ and music education in graduate studies program at Ohio State University	*1955*	
Taught music K-12 in Wakeman, Ohio as first black teacher in this School district	*1956*	
Studied organ and other instruments privately at the Oberlin Conservatory		

Served as Band Director and *1958*
vocal music instructor at George
Washington Carver Four County
Regional High School in Culpepper, Virginia

Awarded Master of Music Education Degree from Pennsylvania
State University

Served as substitute teacher in the *1960*
Philadelphia School District

Served as Choir Master, played
organ and integrated Lafayette
Hills Methodist Church. Played
organ for Mother Bethel A.M.E.
Church in Philadelphia, located on
the oldest parcel of land owned by
African-Americans, purchased by
Richard Allen.

Taught elementary school music *1962*
in Millville, New Jersey, to 1500
students, weekly.

Taught K-6 music at Friends *1965*
Select in Philadelphia

Taught 5-7 grade vocal music at *1966*   Attended performance of *Tann-*
Lawrenceville Intermediate School   *hauser* at the Metropolitan Opera
in Lawrenceville, New Jersey   and had lunch with Richard Wag-
                                        ner's granddaughter, Friedelind

Served as Adjunct Professor of Music Education at Trenton State College, now named the College of New Jersey	*1966*	
Trained music education student teachers from Westminster Choir College (1967-1980)	*1967*	Purchased house on Hamilton Street in Powelton Village in Philadelphia
	1980	Traveled throughout England, Wales, France, and Ireland
	1981	Spent the summer on Nantucket Island
	1982	Traveled throughout England, Germany, Switzerland, and France
Retired from Lawrenceville School District	*1991*	Served as the first black House Manager at the Walnut Street Theater for one season
	1994	My Mother, Beatrice Banks Cole, died
	1995	Served as Chair of the Greater Philadelphia Volunteer Committee of the Philadelphia Orchestra
	1996	Traveled to West Africa and was introduced to Lamin Darboe and Jallomon Konteh by Chuck Davis and became their sponsor

	1996	Served as Chair of the Board of the Settlement Music School West Philadelphia Branch
	1998	Traveled to Africa
	1999	Traveled to India and Nepal for a month
	2000	Sponsored Lamin's resettlement to the USA to study in Philadelphia
		Mrs. Ella B. Couch became my "surrogate" Mother and inspired many of the poems through her many years of living
Met my long lost Merriweather niece and nephew	*2004*	
	2008	Traveled to South America
	2010	Inducted into the Humboldt, Tennessee, "Hall of Fame"
		Served as Grand Marshal for the Strawberry Festival in Humboldt, Tennessee
		Aunt Pearl Banks Elliot, my last surviving immediate family member, died

Muhammed Jallow surrogtate grandson born in The Gambia, West Africa	*2012*	
Lamin Darboe and Darcel Haynes are married in Philadelphia, PA	*2014*	
Sarjo Konteh surrogate granddaughter born in The Gambia, West Africa	*2015*	Traveled to Oslo, Norway, to hear Musa Ngqungwana sing the role of Zuniga in the opera, *Carmen*
	2016	First American grandson, Essah Darboe, born in Philadelphia, PA

≈ My Mother ≈
Beatrice Banks Cole

My mother was cooking for her family on the farm when she was six years old. She had to stand on a tomato box to reach the stove. She lived with her father, stepmother and two daughters, my mother's half sisters, on an eighty acre farm outside of Humboldt, Tennessee. My mother's stepmother treated her daughters, the half sisters, like royalty, while she made my mother do most of the cooking and cleaning around the house.

My grandmother, Lucy Cora Lee Simmons, died when my mother was three years old. My grandfather, Robert Banks, had share croppers to help work his farm and was a controlling force in the town of Humboldt.

My mother was very smart, but her education stopped when she finished 10th grade. At that time Stigall School, the colored public school in Humboldt, Tennessee, only went to 10th grade and students had to go to Tennessee State in Nashville to get a high school diploma. That's what my aunts did, but my mother was not allowed to finish high school because she worked on the farm and later in town as a domestic worker for the George Bailey family.

My grandparents saw to it that my mother married my father because he had a store in this little town of Humboldt. So my mother married him, certainly to get away from that household. She was in her 20s probably when she got married and there were years difference in my mother's and father's ages.

My mother always stressed education to me. She always said: "You're going to school and you're going to learn." I was punished if I didn't study. Even with my piano playing, I would be practicing when I could hear the other children outside playing. I'd tell my mother that I would like to go out to play and sometimes my father would try to intercede for me: "Oh, let the boy go out and play," but my mother told him he'd better get out of the house, otherwise he knew what he would get. So my mother was dominant in that household. She ran a tight ship. I guess she got that from her stepmother.

My mother lived through me. For her entire life, she never stopped wanting piano lessons and more schooling. When she died, she regretted that she never accomplished those things. She always talked about how badly she was treated. Sometimes fate leaves us suspended in mid-air. The breezes never release us; however, we keep going.

≈ My Father ≈

William Bonaparte Cole

I called my father "Mr. Cole" because my mother called him Mr. Cole.

During my early childhood, my father had a general store in Humboldt, Tennessee. Sometimes he worked in Memphis on the boats as a stevedore and I wouldn't see him for maybe a month. When he did return home, I would run from him. I supposed, "Out of sight, soon forgotten."

When I was a small boy, my father would take me to the barber shop across the railroad tracks and he would tell the people in the barber shop: "My boy can read this newspaper" and they would say: "Oh no, he can't."

I would read what was on the printed page in front of me. They would give me a penny or a nickel for my performance. My trick for the day was completed. My father was proud of his son.

Before I left my home for college, my father had stopped working on the ships, so he was around more and I got to know him better. Our difference did not keep us from loving one another very much.

≈ My Upbringing ≈

I grew up in Humboldt, Tennessee, a small town in west Tennessee. Maybe on a good day, there were 8 or 9 thousand people in this little town of Humboldt. I grew up there with my mother and my father and my mother's grandmother, Lucy F. Yancy (see page 74), who lived to be 110 years of age. My great grandmother became my brother and my sister because I was the only child born to my parents. I enjoyed playing tricks on her.

My mother's name was Beatrice Banks Cole. My father was William Bonaparte Cole.

Our house in the town of Humboldt was on an acre of land. We were the only black people in town who had indoor toilets at that time. We lived three doors from the Stigall School. My father used his influence with the wealthiest man in town to let us hook up with the school's sewer system. Most people in the area did not have indoor facilities until later.

This was during the time of segregation when things were separate and unequal. We, as a people, did learn how to overcome, and that we did with a great amount of dignity.

≈ My Music Training ≈

There were not that many people of color in the little town of Humboldt who knew much about music. Mrs. Edna Mae Spearman and Sarah Jeffries were considered good "piano players." I took piano lessons mostly with Mrs. Edna Mae Spearman (see page 83), who was the grandniece of William Grant Still, the famous African-American composer. I would have a scheduled lesson with Mrs. Spearman for Tuesday after school, but she was never dependable. If somebody else offered to take her to Memphis that day or to some other place, she would take the best offer. Mrs. Spearman would tell me: "I can't give you a lesson today." I'd go home to tell my mother and she would say: "Robert, where's Mrs. Spearman?" I'd say: "She couldn't give me a lesson today." So Mama would say: "Go back and tell her that I made dinner and I cooked collard greens, neck bones, sweet potato pie, cornbread, and macaroni and cheese." Before I could get back home, I might stop and talk with some kids, Mrs. Spearman would be there sitting in her usual place at our dining room table. She loved to eat. She was a bit overweight. My mother would pay one dollar for the lessons. Sometimes Mama would make her take the money. I suppose she felt guilty about eating the food and taking the money too. That's how I got my music lessons.

Years later, I played piano at Mrs. Spearman's funeral. She had moved to the Philadelphia area to be with some of her family. I was called and asked to play at her funeral in Camden, New Jersey in May, 1984.

≈ My Music ≈

The thing I remember most about listening to my music was the Mormon Tabernacle Choir half-hour radio broadcast every Sunday morning. It always came on at the same time I was supposed to be leaving the house to go to Sunday school at St. James Baptist Church. I remember a lot of times I would put my shoes on and then take them off to lengthen the time it took for me to get dressed so that I could hear the entire broadcast. My mother would be yelling: "Aren't you ready yet? You better hurry up and get out of there," and I'd take a shoe off and put it on again. I timed it so that the choir (200 voices, I think) would be just about be going off when I finally was leaving the house.

My mother would always threaten me with a whipping if I didn't hurry up and get to church, a fifteen minute walk from our house. That's the main thing I remember about hearing good music in Humboldt at that time of my childhood. As a youngster in Humboldt, I guess that was sort of the beginning of that "classically trained" music thing that made such a big impression on me. Frank Asper would be at the organ and he would always play a little short prelude or interlude. Sometimes I would be "playing" along with him on the table in my room. Then my mother would come to the door to see how well dressed I was, so quickly I'd start buttoning up my shirt or putting on the shoe I had removed earlier. Then she'd come back and realize that: "Boy, you had those shoes on before. I'm going to whip you good tonight. You better hurry up and get out of here."

Of course, in Sunday School, they were talking about, shall we say, nothing. Sometimes they'd spend a whole half hour talking about Moses and the burning bush and would argue about whether the bush was really burning (smile). I thought it was strange thinking at my early age.

I wanted to be listening to the Mormon Tabernacle Choir. The singing was awesome and the organ playing was fulfilling. I was impressed with those harmonic sounds. I'd never heard an organ playing on such a grand scale as the Tabernacle organ was used. Since that time, I was drawn to the organ and went on to become the first organ major graduate at what was then Tennessee State College.

≈ My "Other Family" ≈
The Bailey Robinson Lewis Family

My mother worked as a domestic in that household. They were "good people," as the saying goes. To this day, a number of years later, I still am in contact with some members of that family who remain in Humboldt. The boys in that family were my playmates and I would go to their house to play and at other times they would come to my house to play. My mother's grandmother had also worked for that family, the Bailey clan, who were prominent people in Humboldt. There is still a Bailey Park there today that I was never allowed to play in when I lived there, but now it is open to everyone.

I heard talk that my mother's stepmother's father could have been a member of the Bailey clan. My grandmother had a saying: "Be nice to everybody because you don't know who you are kin to."

≈ My Place ≈

In Humboldt, you had bathrooms for colored. You had white drinking fountains and black drinking fountains. Colored, they would say. Colored. I was brought up in such a way that I always knew who I was and knew what I needed to do. My mother saw to it that I knew that. I knew my place at that time of my life. I was told in growing up, "If I ever hear of you doing this or that…," I knew what was expected of me in order to survive in that environment.

Since I knew what was expected from me, I found it much easier to conform to those expectations, rather than to rebel and risk punishment. Sparing the rod and spoiling the child was not the rule in my household.

≈ My Church ≈

In that part of west Tennessee, you were either Baptist, Methodist or sanctified (evangelical), with Baptist being the dominant community in the South at that time. We belonged to St. James Baptist Church. They were rather progressive in their way of thinking. The music at St. James did not include many spirituals, you see. They were trying to erase the suffering from that earlier slave mentality. As far as they were concerned, the Civil War never happened and everyone was trying to forget the place of truth in that era of history.

I was invited back to play organ recitals at that church after I had gone off to Tennessee State. I am forever indebted to the St. James congregation for their financial support and for helping me achieve many of the goals that my mother had mapped out for me.

≈ My Education ≈

I was reading when I was three years old. My mother taught me at home at a very early age. I started school in the second grade. I'd stay in a grade maybe a half a year and they would move me to another grade level because I could add and read and I got bored easily. As a result, I finished high school when I was sixteen.

My schooling was at Stigall High School in Humboldt, which was not integrated and was separate and truly unequal. The books in our school came from the white schools. Pages were torn out. You'd go to read a passage and your book would be missing the page.

All the Stigall students went to school in July and August and the first two weeks of September. From September to December, there was no school because the Stigall students picked cotton in the fall and strawberries in the spring. That meant that we were usually in school during the hottest days of the year at a time when there was no such thing as air conditioning in the school.

Sometimes school would open again in December. I remember many times my grandfather would go to the Superintendent of Schools, whose name was also Cole (not related), and, he would say: "Mr. Cole, I don't have all my crops in and here's a ham I brought you," and so there would be an announcement the next day that school wouldn't start up again until January. Then we'd be in classes from January to possibly May.

Our school usually didn't open during June because that was the time to pick strawberries. The uptown schools didn't have that schedule. They would start in September and go straight through to June.

I was driven to learn due to my mother's determination for me to succeed. I could not tell her I didn't have any homework. My mother would say: "What did you do today in school? Ok, we're going to do it over." So I had to go over with her what I'd learn that day. Many times, I'd be the only one who would have done the homework and sometimes I couldn't explain how I got it, but I always had my work. My mother would see to that.

I only lived three doors from the school, so the teachers were always reporting on what Robert did today and what Robert didn't do. It was "tell on Robert" time.

I was sixteen years old when I graduated from Stigall High School. All along, my mother was planning for me to go to college. There was no question about that. The emphasis would be on music at Tennessee State College at that time, now, Tennessee State University in Nashville, Tennessee.

≈ My College Experience ≈

When I went to Tennessee State, I was sixteen years old. I was awestruck. It was the first time I had been that far away from home because my parents never let me out of their sight.

It was interesting handling my new space. So many new things to see and learn. Finances were a problem because my father died in my second year at Tennessee State College. My mother had to make all the provisions to borrow money to pay my tuition.

To help with finances for the first three years, I worked for a lawyer and his wife in Nashville, Attorney R. B. J. Campbell and his wife, Margaret Campbell who was a librarian at Tennessee State. I worked for them cleaning their house. That was sort of my home away from home. Attorney and Mrs. Campbell helped to reshape my thinking. When it was time to get paid, Mrs. Campbell would tell me to go talk to her husband. I'd have to sit down and tell him what I had done that week and why I should get paid. Sometimes thirty minutes later, I'd still be there explaining why I needed the money that was owed me. It wasn't that much money anyway. He brought me out of my shell. He was doing his lawyer number on me. It was good in many ways. He taught me to speak up for myself.

One of the things I always remember about Tennessee State is that on every third Sunday, there would be chapel service for the students in the afternoon. This one Sunday, Dr. Benjamin Mays, President of Morehouse College, came to speak. I'll never forget it. I was in awe of this man. And his theme for that time was "Goodbye God, I'm going to college." I will always remember Dr. Mays and that sermon.

My music teachers at Tennessee State were a work in progress. They spent more time fighting with one another than helping students succeed. My organ teacher, John H. Sharpe, also was a good friend. Many times, my organ teacher told me to take a class and the department head would say: "You don't need that." This type of fighting and infighting still goes on today in the academic world. The department head obviously enjoyed torturing students to show off his knowledge of any subject. The first time around I flunked his music theory class, so I took it over again and did a little better. In the music department at that time, there were only eight teachers and about twenty students. It was a small department just getting started.

As a matter of fact, it took me five years to graduate. I finished in 1952 with a Bachelor's in Music. There are many firsts in my life and I was the first organ major to graduate from the school.

≈ My Life in Nashville ≈

One advantage of going to Tennessee State was that Fisk University was nearby in Nashville. One summer, I lived on the Fisk campus with Mrs. and Reverend W. S. Ellington, who had served as Pastor for the First Baptist Church in Nashville and who was nationally known for his "Prodigal Son" sermon. Being on campus gave me a chance to hear wonderful music, including the Fisk Jubilee Singers, organ music of note, and choir singing equal to that of the Mormon Tabernacle Choir, whose radio broadcasts I grew up with. The first time I heard the Bach *Magnificat* was at Fisk. I'd never heard anything like it before in my life.

One summer I played organ for services at the First Baptist Church in Nashville with Helen Work, who was the choir director and the sister of eminent composer, John W. Work.

I had the pleasure last spring of going back to Nashville. One of my mentees graduated from Meharry Medical School, which is just across the street from Fisk. I was able to go back to Nashville and look at the campus and visit some of the places I had been, although I hardly knew them because the whole area had changed. I spent many Sundays at the chapel at Fisk when I was a student at Tennessee State College.

Charles Spurgeon Johnson, the President of Fisk at the time, had been part of the Harlem Renaissance and he brought other Renaissance artists to Nashville. Arna Bontemps was there. Langston Hughes. Aaron Douglas. What a place! They always had an arts festival in the springtime of the year. Anybody who was anybody in culture came to Fisk for this arts festival and they all expanded my world.

≈ My Marching Band ≈

I always wanted to play in a marching band since I saw the marching band practicing at the other high school in Humboldt. The boys in the shop class at Stigall High School worked at the uptown school for training in shop for a letter grade. The shop teacher took 5 or 6 boys to strip and refinish the stadium bleachers and other things as part of our hands-on training in woodworking.

We could see the band practicing on the football field as we were sanding and fixing the bleachers. I would spend most of my time looking at the band, as my grade reflected. I figured out a way to do the minimum amount of work for that class. I never had an idea that one day I would be playing in the band at Tennessee State. I played the bass drum and just had to keep the beat: boom, boom, boom. One excitement was the time our marching band played at the Kentucky Derby. That was really something for a country boy to see.

≈ My First Music Job ≈

When I finished Tennessee State, I had two job offers: one in Saint Louis and one in Mississippi. Itta Bena, Mississippi in the Delta. The Campbells, for whom I had worked in Nashville and who became my confidantes, thought that I certainly didn't have any business at nineteen years of age going off to Saint Louis; however, Itta Bena was not the best beginning for a young teacher starting out. No school supplies and modest living conditions. Whatever we needed, the parents would sell whatever they could to raise money to buy instruments or music or uniforms for the band.

Most people in the community were happy having a Band Director because the band gave the students some exposure in the community. Itta Bena was even smaller than Humboldt. Cotton fields for days. I was happy after being there about four months when my induction orders came through to serve two years in the Army. The people there were nice people. Some were sharecroppers and farmers with good intentions. It was just farms and cotton fields. The students were eager to learn. For the most part, they were going to do what they had to do or what I made them do and soon they would be raising a family and being a part of the system. That was the setup that was put before them. I was happy to try another venue at that time in my life.

≈ My Army Training ≈

After having been drafted, my Army training was at Fort Jackson, South Carolina. I was in the band there. I think at that time it was somewhat integrated. I don't remember what I played in the band. I might have carried the tuba which was all metal and must have weighed at least ten pounds. Oh, my God, it was heavy! Today they are mostly made of plastic. I carried it instead of playing it most times because I was always looking for interesting people and wonderful things to be seen.

To this day, my mind is open to new ideas and experiences and a love for good people. Coming from Humboldt made me observant of everything around: buildings, people, cars, trucks. I just had to see all that I could. I have noticed this awareness in my grandson, Essah. At four months old, he is watchful and appears to be noticing everything around him. It pays to take note of what is around you; therefore, it is in the choosing that will follow you forever.

≈ My World Expanded ≈

My Army unit finally arrived in Korea. I was assigned to be a chaplain's assistant and ended up mostly playing a little pump organ during services in the field of battle. The chaplain was happy to have me and another assistant to work with him.

I loved walking around and experiencing the sights, sounds, and aromas in Korea. I visited many places of culture while overseas.

I had the pleasure of visiting Japan and that was even more interesting. I wanted to hear the NHK Symphony Orchestra in Tokyo. The ticket sellers would see me coming with my soldier's uniform on and they would say: "Sold out," and of course, I wouldn't hear it. I would say: "I want to speak to the manager." The manager would come out and I would say: "I've come this far and I am a musician and I want to hear the orchestra. Now what can you do for me?" I would always get in.

I saw the Kabuki theater in Tokyo. I didn't know what it was about at that time, but it was fascinating and most enjoyable. I even went to a Christian church there. I think it might have been a Japanese Presbyterian church. I heard the hymn *God So Love the World* sung in English by Japanese Christians. It was wonderful. I took the train to Kamakura where the big Diabutsu is. (see page 84) I spent the day roaming around the grounds and just soaking up the culture. I ate in Japanese restaurants. I just had a wonderful time.

I would always go to the big department stores and buy things to send my mother. By nature, I am a "shopaholic." When I finally came home from overseas, she would have all of these things, china and kimonos and things that I had sent her, and she would never use them or wear them. Every summer, she'd hang them outside to air out and then she'd put them back in the trunk and put tobacco in it to keep the moths out. I guess she didn't know about mothballs. Of course, the tobacco stained everything.

Touring in Japan was a wonderful experience. That got me interested in wanting to see the world and to realize that there was more out there than what I'd grown up seeing in Humboldt, Tennessee.

≈ My Time in Columbus ≈

When I got out of the Army after the Korean conflict, I was home less than four days when I got my clothes together and was off to Columbus, Ohio. I knew no one there and I arrived on a Saturday when Ohio State was playing Michigan at the football stadium. Here I was: this country Tennessee boy with this big suitcase probably tied with ropes around it. The taxicab driver said: "I'll let you out here, but I'm not going over there." The crowd was impossible to compete with. So he let me out among the throngs of people going to the football game at the stadium. I just followed them lugging this suitcase. I guess they thought: "There's a country bumpkin. He's here to work in the dormitory or something."

I had no idea where I was going to stay. Everyone appeared to be going to the stadium, so that's where I ended up. My first experience there was with some students who lived in the stadium dorm (the stadium had a dormitory connected to it), and I asked them: "Where do you go to sign up for classes at the administration building?" and they said: "Nothing's open today, but you can stay with us until Monday." So I stayed there until Monday morning. What an experience! At that time, one could believe in people. There are still a few good ones yet around.

I found a place to live in the city of Columbus that was quite an experience too. I stayed there for the year. It was affordable and the GI Bill gave me enough money to survive, barely.

I went to Ohio State for learning. After my time in the

Army, I realized that my previous education had been limited and that I needed to get somewhere to improve on my basic education. I chose Columbus because the other chaplain's assistant in the Army with me had gone to Ohio State University.

At Ohio State, I was in music education and studied with Joseph Leeder who had written the definitive book on teaching junior high music in public schools. He wrote the book with Frances Andrews of Pennsylvania State University and over the years, I studied with both of them.

I took several other classes at Ohio State and did some keyboard work with Wilbur Held, the famous organist. I did more organ playing there in one month than I did in four years before.

Dr. Held was a very thorough teacher. I did my best playing at Ohio State. I haven't done that well since. He was an understanding man. I saw him years later and I thanked him and gave him an apology for not doing better. He said: "Under the circumstances, you did very well." He was very supportive. Just a kind man.

The out of state fee per class hour at Ohio State was exorbitant, so I couldn't stay there too long. Even with the veterans' assistance, it was very difficult.

In the meantime, I just practiced and studied. That was the beginning of my new learning mode for advancement of myself.

≈ My Time in Wakeman ≈

In 1955, I had to get some money coming in, so I took a job in Wakeman, Ohio. This was a teaching job for grades K-12. It's a small town, not far from Columbus and close to Oberlin, Ohio. At Oberlin I took special classes: independent study of instruments of the band and orchestra with Arthur Williams. After teaching my music students all day, in the evening I also took organ classes with a teacher there.

Wakeman was not an integrated community. There were two other black people in the town: the barber and his sister. I stayed with them. So with me, it made three blacks in the town of Wakeman, Ohio. This was in the fifties. This was another first for me and for them.

I was the band director at the high school. There were probably 150 people in the high school, but they had a football team like all Ohio schools had. Football was the thing. Four or five of the kids who played in the band played football too. If the football coaches were not happy with me for that week, they wouldn't let the football players change into their band uniforms for the half-time performance. I never knew when the coaches would cooperate. That was quite an experience in Wakeman, Ohio.

I don't recall too many incidents and I didn't go looking for them. I did go into Cleveland for cultural activities. Wakeman was maybe 50 miles from Cleveland. I went into Cleveland for a bit of culture, but not often because money at that time was scarce for me. That was my Wakeman, Ohio experience. I was there 1955-1956.

≈ My Time in Culpepper ≈

From Wakeman, Ohio, I went to Culpepper, Virginia, because I got a higher salary. I had the marching band, the choir and I taught general music classes.

Here I was back in the South. The schools were not integrated yet. This was 1956-1958. This was a black regional high school and the kids came in from four counties: Orange, VA; Culpepper, VA; Rappohonock, VA; and Madison, VA. This was the George Washington Carver Four County Regional High School. I was in charge of vocal and instrumental music for grades 9-12. The marching band was very good. The band was the Cadillac of the school. We got to march at all the festivals in the area because those little towns in Virginia were trying to show that they were open to everyone and had included Carver Marching Band in their parades.

There was another high school marching band in our town that had more pricey instruments than what Carver's band had. My trouble there was that after the first year, I went to see the school superintendent to tell him that I needed a budget. I mentioned that the school district had supplied instruments and other supplies to the other school, but at Carver, the parents had to raise all the money for band supplies and instruments. We needed more money from the school district to purchase instruments. So he said: "Well, I'll tell you, Cole, what I'm going to do. I'm going to give you $150." I said: "Thank you. That won't even buy one music score, but I'll take it."

My principal, Harvey Fleshman, was not pleased that I had gone to the superintendent. He invited me into his office to let me know that the superintendent had called him and told him about my visit. The principal said to me: "If you do that again, I'll have to let you go." I was pretty "headstrong" at that time. Thank God I'm not as demanding now. *[Some people would argue that point.]*

I said: "No, you won't have to let me go. I will quit." So I stayed for the rest of the year, but after that I left after two or three years at the school.

I was always there for my students. Some members of the marching band formed a little dance band and played gigs on the side. The principal informed me that instruments from the school could not be "loaned" and that the students couldn't use them for their little band. I allowed the students to continue to use whatever they needed. The instruments were purchased by the parents and not the school district. My students still remember little things like that and they're grateful that I was always for them.

We had a wonderful marching band. We played for football games and marched in parades in the area. We were always invited to play in the Apple Blossom Festival parade in Winchester, Virginia. That was a big parade

There were lessons taught at that parade. One student was one of the best drummers in the band, but always marched to the beat of his own drum. One time he didn't do what I'd asked him to do, so I relieved him of his duties with the band. He didn't speak to me for maybe a month or two afterwards, but he went to the Apple Blossom parade to see us mess up because the band had all kinds of difficult steps to do like stop freezing, turning about face and going the other way on certain counts. John went to see us mess up, but the kids performed better than ever. So his comment to me was: "Old man, you taught me a lesson." To this day, if you were to talk to him, he'll say: "He taught me a lesson. One monkey doesn't stop the show."

Where I stayed in Culpepper was interesting. The superintendent for the regional high school had about five houses around the school that he rented out. If you got the job as a teacher, you were going to rent one of his houses from him. You had to stay in one of his houses. There were some teachers who lived in Culpepper or Orange who stayed at home, but his apartments had to be filled first when hiring new teachers. They would hire an outsider before they took someone from the area to teach there. That was quite a little operation, I'd say.

I am in contact with my Culpepper students from yesteryear as of this writing. There was much love shared with those students.

≈ My Jobs in Philadelphia ≈

I came back to Philadelphia and got a room at the Y on Arch Street, where I stayed for three or four years. In the summer, I took jobs as camp counselor or things like that. That's when I went to Nantucket and worked for one summer. I ran the elevator at the Y on Arch Street for a short time. It helped pay the bills until I became versed in how to fill out the forms and applications for employment with the Board of Education. I got a job as a substitute teacher in Philly and I taught there from 1958-1960. I taught history, English, and whatever was needed.

A permanent position was offered to teach music at the Catto School in Philadelphia. Catto was a school for "problem" boys. That was quite an experience. Three years is all you'd want in a school like that. It was demanding and I was determined that they would learn.

I taught general music. It took special planning to keep the boys interested in formal learning.

During this time, I moved to stay with Edna and Bill Griffin, who were my hosts for about three years in West Philadelphia. Edna Griffin was the first black woman to be President of the Philadelphia Teachers Association and was quite high up in the National Education Association. Her husband's business was Rogers Travel Agency, which took many teachers to Europe and Africa. They grew me up and "schooled me" in city living.

≈ My Time in Millville ≈

My next stop was Millville, New Jersey, where I taught elementary school music. I covered five schools and met with about 5,000 students each week, pushing the piano from room to room. It was not a good experience. I was there from 1960-1962. The experience helped me grow up quickly and learn that there is no substitute for dedication and commitment for imparting knowledge.

I stayed in Millville with Mrs. Delina Shepherd. She was very special to me and a positive influence in my life.

≈ My Friends @ Friends Select ≈

After Millville, I went to Friends Select in Philadelphia simply because the job had less movement. I was teaching music in the elementary school K-6. There might have been one other black teacher before me, but when they moved to the Parkway, I was the first black teacher at that school. It was a Quaker experience and not much money earned. I think I had a music budget less than $100. My salary was $3000 for the year, if I remember correctly.

After teaching in a Quaker school, I was not drawn to Quakerism. The thing I did like was the quietness imparted to all.

I still hear from some of my students and they all have become my extended family including their grown-up sons and daughters.

≈ LUNCH WITH LANGSTON HUGHES ≈

Through my Quaker experience at Friends Select, I became a friend of Helen Morgan Brooks who was a writer of poetry and a Quaker of African descent. She lived in Poweltown Village where I was living at the time and was a friend of Langston Hughes. She was having Langston to lunch and invited me. He was a very gracious man, a cordial man. At that time, I wasn't quite sure who Langston Hughes was. It wasn't until about 10 years later that I realized that I had been in the company of a great writer. I had no thorough history of my people growing up in Humboldt, Tennessee. I didn't know much about the Harlem Renaissance either. That learning came later in my life.

≈ My House in Powelton Village ≈

After having lived with Edna and William E. Griffin and Bill's father in West Philadelphia, I said to William Senior: "Pop, I'm thinking of moving to my own apartment." He gave me encouragement to do it. So I went looking. I liked the area of Powelton Village because the trees and the gardens reminded me of Humboldt, Tennessee. I got an apartment on Hamilton Street at number 3617. It was a one-room apartment. It had a small galley kitchen and a bathroom. I was there five years or more.

Across the street lived Mervin Hutton who was a musician and a music teacher at Westtown Friends School. He had always wanted to be a conductor, so he decided he was going to Vienna, Austria to study conducting. Before he left, he said: "I'm selling my house for 10,000 dollars." I said: "I'd like to buy it." I didn't have any money, but I knew I could get loans. My friend, Jacob Wortham, who wrote for *Black Enterprise* and the *Village Voice* said: "If you like it, why not get it?"

That's how I got the house in Powelton, 3614 Hamilton Street, a Victorian from about 1850. I was so interested in the well-being of my neighbors, who would come to me with their tales, that finally I earned the title of "The Mayor." Because I was a hoarder, I started the Powelton Village Porch Sale to get rid of some of my "shop-a-holic" purchases. That mushroomed into the big Powelton Village Porch Sale that still goes on today. The neighbors would put things out on their porches and the sidewalk. Now people come from all over and rent space to sell all kinds of things on the first Saturday after Labor Day. Oren Reid was working for the *Philadelphia Bulletin* in the early years of the Sale, and she came to interview me about how to run a porch sale. When I moved in, the neighborhood was on its way back from a serious decline. It was a neighborhood of mostly people of Irish descent at that time. There were no more than a half dozen or a dozen black people living in Powelton at that time. Regardless of that, everybody got along.

There were apartments in my house at 3614 Hamilton Street. After a while, I had a bed and breakfast there. It went very well because I was able to get a steady stream of guests who were coming to the University of Pennsylvania or Drexel University to teach for a semester.

I hold fond memories of Powelton Village in West Philadelphia, Pennsylvania.

≈ My Time with Paul Robeson ≈

Charlotte Bell was a friend who had done some piano accompaniment for Paul Robeson's recitals. She was a member of the Varick AME Church, where we met and became friends. Charlotte introduced me to Paul Robeson and his sister and caregiver, Marian Forsythe. Mr. Robeson had an extraordinary career as an opera singer, Broadway and movie star, and political activist. Charlotte asked me to take them to hear the Philadelphia Oratorio Choir at First Baptist Church. They sang an oratorio every Sunday. What a joy! It became a regular routine. After the concert, we'd go back to Charlotte's house to have ice cream and cake. Then I'd take Mr. Robeson and Mrs. Forsythe home to Walnut Street in West Philadelphia where he was living at that time.

At the concert, I was not at liberty to tell anybody who Mr. Robeson was. We just sat and listened. He would only answer you if you talked to him. He was peaceful and quiet at all times. I knew a few things about his life. It was much later, after I read the Duberman biography of him, that I realized what he had gone through. He was very docile at this time of his life. You'd think he was contemplating something. I think he lived maybe four or five years after we stopped attending those oratorio concerts. During our years together, he was calm, peaceful and well cared for.

≈ My Final Teaching Position ≈
Lawrenceville, New Jersey

From Friends Select School, I went to Lawrenceville, New Jersey public schools. I got to Lawrenceville thanks to a friend of mine, Michael Rothstein, who lived in Philadelphia and was an administrator in the school system in Lawrenceville. They were looking to integrate staff and students in the middle school.

By the time classes were to begin that fall, the new middle school, where I was to teach, had not been completed, so we had classes at the Armory with portable partitions between the classes. Trying times! On the first day of class I thought: "What have I gotten involved in?"

I retired from there after 22 years of commuting from Philadelphia to Lawrenceville, New Jersey.

I was the first teacher to integrate the middle school in the district. They had a few black teachers in the elementary schools and maybe two black teachers in the high school. Lawrenceville was not a racially diverse community at that time, but had a mixture of economic levels. For the most part, the students were ready and eager to learn.

There was a strong music program in the system. Even in the middle school, there were two vocal teachers, two instrumental teachers, and three part-time music teachers just for the middle school. There were three elementary schools in the system and each one of them had its own music teacher.

Every year, I did a winter program and a spring concert. There would be 150, maybe nearly 200 kids singing in the chorus. There were many good student musicians there. Some of them played well enough to accompany my chorus. Several of my former students went on to become concert pianists. One of them sings in the Metropolitan Opera chorus, and one is a media executive active in various cultural venues.

At that time, with their parents' permission, I could bring a group of my students to visit Philadelphia. Any weekend, sometimes I would have as many as five kids in my house with me in Philly. I'd take them to museums, concerts and plays. Friday night we would go to Father Divine's dining room at 36ᵗʰ and Chestnut streets in Philadelphia. Once they met Mother Divine there. She asked one of the students to play the piano for her. She was impressed with all of the students and began to expect to see them at the Divine Tracy Hotel.

A highlight of one of the spring concerts was when Mother Divine and the Rosebuds came in two limousines to the spring concert in Lawrenceville to hear my chorus sing. The students who had eaten in the dining room with her in Philadelphia knew who she was and thanked her for coming.

My stay in Lawrenceville was a pleasant place to end a long teaching career. The memories and many friends made there will remain in my heart forever. I am continually in touch with the students and teachers from the school in Lawrenceville.

≈ The Walnut Street Theater ≈
My Job at America's Oldest Theater

In 1991 I retired from teaching. During that year, I was house manager at the Walnut Street Theater. I got the job because I knew one of the readers of new plays for the theater. She knew I was retiring and they needed a house manager, so she referred me to the director of the theater. I was the first minority house manager in the long history of the Walnut Street Theater. I had not been involved in such a large arena for the arts before, and the challenge was most satisfying.

I would go to work at 9:00 a.m. in the morning and leave at 1:00 a.m. the next morning. I set up programs that are still being used today. The ushers were strictly volunteers and I initiated a procedure to track them for each performance. I took care of the schedule for the ushers, the concession stands and the bars. It was a big, big responsibility for a retiree. There are people from the Walnut Street Theater who keep in contact with me to this day. They appreciated what I did at the Theater.

≈ The Philadelphia Orchestra ≈
My Volunteer Work

In 1995, I chaired one of the volunteer committees for the Philadelphia Orchestra. That was another first for me. At that time, I was also the manager of the Orchestra boutique at the Academy of Music in Philadelphia. There were about 12 volunteer committees that were helping to raise money for the Philadelphia Orchestra. My committee, The Greater Philadelphia Committee, was a hodge-podge of people. As long as they were breathing, we took them into our Committee. During my tenure with the Committee, we accomplished some monumental projects for the Philadelphia Orchestra.

≈ My First Trip to Africa ≈

The reason I went to Africa the first time was because of Chuck Davis, the Director of Dance Africa. After meeting him backstage, I asked him if he would be interested in going to the evening performance of Renee Harris Pure Movement. He was so appreciative that I had asked him to accompany me to this recital. It would have been 1995. We seemed to hit it off from the very beginning. Ever since then, we refer to one another as brothers.

At that point, Chuck had been going to Africa for thirty years or more. He'd go every summer to see different dance forms and glean from them the choreography for Dance Africa. One day, he told me that he was going to Africa and I said: "I'd like to go with you." Then he mentioned that he took care of a family in Africa by sending them money and much needed school supplies. I said: "That's a good idea. I'd like to meet somebody in Africa whom I could help too." He said: "I have just the right family for you." He gave me the names of two young men who lived with their grandmother and uncle in a compound in The Gambia, West Africa. I told him I would like to accompany him on his next trip to Africa. That summer with about twelve dancers and myself, off to Africa we went

In 1996, we flew from New York to Dakar, Senegal, West Africa, and traveled bumpily overland to The Gambia. The Gambia is right in the middle of Senegal—a little strip of land. One of the people on the trip was Renee Harris, whose dance company (Pure Movement) we had seen earlier and who was emerging as a major force in the "hip hop" dance world. We stayed in a big European-style hotel in the city of Dakar before driving overland to Banjul, the capital of The Gambia. In the afternoon or early morning, Chuck would take our group down to the ocean to do dances and exercise our bodies. On the second day, we took a boat to Goree Island where Africans were shipped to America as slaves. Our guide gave us a lecture and a tour of the slave house. We all wept copious tears. I thought: Where did the Banks and Cole names come from? Our people overcame so much and still are trying to shed the problems created during this period of our history.

The next morning we left for the city of Banjul, which is the capital of The Gambia. On the trip to Banjul, we passed many huts and bumps and police collecting bribes which was all unbelievable. We'd go five miles on asphalt road and then cut off and go across a field when the road was no longer there. We arrived at Bari Village where we got the boat to go over to Banjul. At the pier, we saw boys diving for the coins that people threw in the water.

We arrived in Banjul and went to the Bungalow Beach Hotel. Each morning before breakfast, we went to the beach to do our warm up exercises and praise God for our stay in Africa. Each day, we'd also have a session with Adele Sach, an ex-pat from Pittsburgh who had married a barrister and was living in The Gambia. She would tell us what to see and what to expect when we went on excursions in the area.

We toured a mosque, went on a fishing boat, saw dancing everywhere, and participated in Africa life as we were instructed. Chuck had arranged for us to go to a concert at the home of Modo Suso, who is an internationally known musician who played a balafon accompanied with drums and singing. One night we went to a naming ceremony at the Suso compound where they gave each member of our group an African name. This was an intense, reflective, and authentic African experience. The name given to me was "Muhammadu Suso."

Banjul is like any other African city. It has crowded streets with aggressive drivers. The big attraction was Serekunda, the big market place. Everyone comes to the market at some point during the day. Everything revolves around the market.

In Africa, I didn't feel stressed by the crowds. When I realized how things worked in Africa, I started taking everything as it came. "No problem," the Africans would say. If something was supposed to happen at ten o'clock in the morning and it didn't happen until seven o'clock that evening, that would be fine. If it didn't happen until the next day, that would be fine too. One time we left at 9:00 a.m. to rush to get to someone's house for a baby naming ceremony. Since we got there so early, I went around to the back and I saw a goat hung up to drain blood from it, and the animal was to be cooked later. I went back inside and told everyone that I wasn't feeling well, so I took a cab back to the hotel. The rest of the group came in around 10 o'clock that night, after they had spent the day and evening at the baby naming ceremony. There was no urgency. I found that approach to life to be very peaceful. Another peaceful moment was when I met the family of my boys: Lamin Darboe and Hamady Konteh. I have since added another surrogate son to this list: Edrissa Jallow.

≈ My African Sons ≈

On August 8, 1996 at 5:30pm, in the compound, I met Lamin Darboe and his cousin, Hamady Jallamon Konteh. In my travel diary I wrote: "Wow! What an experience." I liked them very much on first meeting. They lived in Bundun in a very modest house with other people. Lamie's father died when he was three, so his grandmother, Tomaring Konteh, and his uncle, Jatta Darboe, took care of him.

When I was there, Lamie's grandmother would go about telling everybody that her American son was visiting and was showing off all the gifts I brought for the family.

My friend, Chuck Davis, had been helping the family by paying for their schooling. I took over and started paying for Lamie to attend Saint Augustine, a private Episcopal school in Banjul and for Hamady to attend the local public schools. When I met them, I told them that if they did well in school, I would bring them to America to study.

The difference in the two boys was noticeable. Lamie would study from midnight until early in the morning, Hamady would try to study in the evening with all the kids running around. He was devoted to taking care of the children.

Most days I took the boys to the market and bought them everything they wanted and some things they didn't want. I'd also bring them to swim in the pool at the hotel. They'd have lunch and dinner with me at the hotel. We also went swimming in the ocean. That might have been the first time they had ever been swimming in the ocean.

When it would be time for Lamie and his family to go to the mosque, Lamie would disappear. When they came back home from the mosque, they'd find him and punish him. The next time, he might be dressed and ready to go with them, but most times after that, he would most likely disappear and they would most likely punish him again. Even then, he was living to his own beat and figuring out things for himself, a positive force in his caring and peaceful life.

To get a visa to come to America to study, you had to have done well in school. Lamie had figured out when to study and how to study, so he did exceptionally well in school. Consequently in the year 2000, I arranged for him to come to Philadelphia to live with me and take classes at Drexel University. Lamie had never flown before and had never been away from home. He made it overland by himself to Dakar, but got stranded at the airport there for a day and a half. I telephoned and asked Moutalla, my physician friend in Dakar, to please go to the airport and check on him. They found him looking scared and hungry, so they took him to their house to feed him and let him freshen up and then took him back to the airport just in time to get his flight to New York. He made it!

It was a caring thing to help him realize his dream of studying and living in America. Lamin is married now and they have a precious son, Essah, who is my first grandchild born in America

≈ My Second Trip to Africa ≈

On the second trip to Africa in 1998, we went to the Jan Jan Jangbury Lodge in Georgetown, West Africa, which was another slave trading city. This lodge was a step back in time. In this lodge, there were monkeys in trees and exotic birds singing. One morning I put some doughnuts on the table and went out to get some coffee. When I came back, the doughnuts were gone. The monkeys had swooped down and taken the doughnuts as soon as they observed that I wasn't there. They had been watching me all along.

After finishing our stay at Jan Jan Jangbury Lodge, our group took a boat trip down the Gambia River, which is a freshwater river, en route to the Bungalow Beach Hotel in Serekunda. On this trip, we saw hippos and baboons and watched people dancing in a little park. A long day it was, but fascinating. The next day, we got ready for the ferry ride to Bungalow Beach in Banjul.

I went to Goree Island again, but it didn't have the same impact that the first visit had.

Our group had the good fortune of having dinner in the home of an African doctor and his family in Dakar. He had been introduced to me by an American who arranged for our connection in Dakar. The doctor called us in The Gambia inviting us over for dinner. This was most enjoyable. The hosts served some of the best fried chicken and ice cream I've ever had in my life. His wife, Hadi, and their kids and some neighbors were there to greet us. There was food, food, and more food. It was like being in an American home for a family reunion. I will never forget that Sunday when were went to Moutalla's house. Since that time, Moutalla has visited here in Philadelphia. He was here doing some extra studies at the University of Pennsylvania.

One day I wanted to go to Goufray, which is the village where Alex Haley found his Africa family in *Roots*. Taking a boat there was a trying experience. We got into the little boat and somebody was bailing out water the whole time we were on the River Gambia. The main reason for going was to meet Beta Kinte, who was related to Alex Haley, with whom I had had dinner. I spent a half hour or more at their compound. I took Lamin and Hamady with me. I went so I could have a visual connection to the places and people in the television series of *Roots*.

The second time in Africa was old hat. It was like going back home. I knew the place and everybody in the neighborhood knew me. They said: "BobCole. BobCole is here." It was Africa, my home away from home. Exciting!

≈ My Trip to India and Nepal ≈

In 1999, I spent a month in India and Nepal. That was the trip of a lifetime. I went with a friend who grew up in India. Another friend of mine, Robert Howard, went with us, so there were three of us in total. India is fascinating. I saw the Ajanta Caves. I saw the Taj Mahal. I saw things that many East Indians have not seen. I was on a plane practically every other day. I did the entire southern part of India. On the Ganges River, I saw bodies being burned and smelled the bodies burning in the city of Kerala. Once when we were on the river, I said to my friend, Mr. Howard: "What is that there?" He said: "What does it look like? It's a body that didn't quite burn." Once east Indians got to the Ganges River, that was the most sacred thing to do.

Then in Nepal, another experience was flying over Mount Everest. We went to stupas to hear the Buddhist monks chanting, which was powerful for my music senses. It was a colorful, exotic, wild and wonderful experience to remember for a lifetime.

There was so much history and symbolism. My favorite was the Temple to the Sun. To go to the airport every other day, we would have to get up at three o'clock to get ahead of the crowds in the streets, the cows and the motorcycles. Once I went on a university campus, and I was surrounded by students. A lot of times, they would think I was African, but I'd say: "No, I'm from America." They would be fascinated and they would be firing questions at me, eager to learn what living in the U.S. was like. I'd love to go back to the area, but I'll wait until it gets a little more stable. I'd like to see the northern part of India.

≈ My Triumphant Return ≈
to Humboldt

I left Humboldt at an early age. Once I went off to college, I've never looked back nor have I been back to Humboldt that much. I did go back to be inducted into the Humboldt Hall of Fame in May, 2010, and to be the Grand Marshal for the Strawberry Festival parade that was quite a meaningful and emotional experience.

This all started one day when I got a telephone call from one of the librarians in Humboldt. She called to ask me if it would be okay if she were to put my name up for consideration for the Humboldt Hall of Fame. I'm not sure how she got my name, but I guessed that she had been talking with my cousin, Robert Banks Elliot, who was living there at the time. I had stayed in touch with his mother, my Aunt Pearl, and she must have told Robert about my professional career and my charity work.

Frankly, I didn't hesitate to accept this honor. A few days later, the librarian called me back to say that I was not only accepted for the Hall of Fame, but also that I had been chosen to serve as the Grand Marshal of the Strawberry Festival parade. I hadn't seen the Strawberry Festival since I was in high school, and here I was being named the Grand Marshal.

When I got that phone call, my emotion was that I wished my mother could have seen this. I wished that my father and great grandmother could have seen this. It was a very emotional time for me.

I went to Humboldt for the induction ceremony. They usually did it in the City Hall, but they moved it to the Methodist church so that I could give a brief piano recital during the ceremony. Here I am in this Methodist church playing on this beautiful grand piano. In earlier times, the only way I could have been in that church was if I were the janitor. That was another emotional experience.

There were three people inducted into the Hall of Fame that day. The other two were white. There was a group of my friends attending that evening who knew me and my family from years past.

The next day, I got up early to be the Marshal of the Strawberry Festival Parade (see photo page 91). That was exciting. I was in a car at the beginning of the parade, waving to everybody. There were a few people who remembered me. It was thrilling just to be there to see the people smiling and waving.

After the Festival, there was a luncheon where the honorees and the Festival organizers were recognized. It was good to see that the group was diverse. For instance, the minister of St. James Baptist Church gave the opening prayer. That was my former home church.

While I was there, I visited my mother's, father's and great grandmother's gravesites at Rosehill in Humboldt Cemetery. Thank God for good memories.

Some of the family that my mother worked for still live in Humboldt. This would be the Bailey clan, Charles and Austin Lewis. There's still a good relationship between us.

I went back to Humboldt to take care of my Aunt Pearl because her son, Robert Banks Elliot, had died earlier. I haven't been back to Humboldt since my Aunt Pearl died. She was my mother's sister and the last living relative of my mother's family. She was my last connection to Humboldt.

≈ The Humboldt "Hall of Fame" ≈
My Thank You Speech

I wish to thank the Humboldt Chamber of Commerce for selecting me for this "Hall of Fame" honor. The word **"Fame"** eludes me however. If it is taken to mean that you treat everyone as you wish to be treated, or to do unto others as you wish them to do unto you, then that's what I am about; therefore, I am grateful to accept this induction into the Hall of Fame with the understanding that it was my Humboldt upbringing which helped me survive many adversities. I knew my mother's Grandmother as a child on 715 Sixth Avenue, Humboldt, Tennessee. My mother, father, and my great grandmother taught me well. The people in all of Humboldt monitored me too.

In all my accomplishments in life, I see reflections of my early training here in Humboldt. I am grateful to have had a most rewarding life and to be able to continue in it with health, intellectual vigor and ever-increasing service in faith.

Thanks to the People of Humboldt for helping me to complete the full circle of life while still living on this earth. This honor I am elated to receive and to be acknowledged for my work in helping others. On this date, May 6, 2010, in Humboldt, Tennessee, I would like to thank you for this kind recognition of me for the many years of hard work, thus, making this world a better place in which to live.

≈ Photo Album ≈

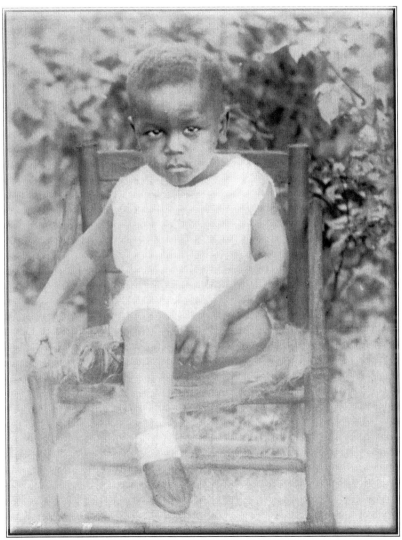

Tennessee Boy at age 3

My Birthplace—Humboldt, Tennessee

My Father—Mr. William Bonaparte Cole

Please accept my sincere congratulations upon your birthday. May good health be yours through many more happy years.

Dwight D. Eisenhower

My Great Grandmother - Lucy Isham Harris at age 100

74   *Tennessee Boy*

Civil War Guns And Television— All In Lifetime

Special to The Commercial Appeal

HUMBOLDT, Tenn., April 9.—A 109-year-old Negro woman, who once received a birthday letter from President Eisenhower, died Saturday afternoon at her home.

Lucy Isham Harris was born a slave on the Gibson County farm of the late John Fitzgerald and her remembrance of those days was still vivid shortly before she died.

She once told of how frightened she was when Union soldiers visited the farm during the Civil War and demanded food. She remembered working in the fields one day and hearing the roar of firing guns.

Despite her age, she never wore glasses and she frequently w a t c h e d television. Married twice, she outlived both husbands and her four children.

She said she attributed her long life to "being unselfish."

My Great Grandmother Remembered

Robert W. Cole   75

My Grandmother - Lucy Cora Simmons

Rob Banks, Colored, Died Last Thursday; Prominent Farmer

Rob. B. Banks, aged 74, prominent Humboldt negro citizen died Thursday morning at 7:45 o'clock at St. Mary's Hospital following a long illness. Banks, one of Gibson County's best known and highly respected colored citizens, was a prosperous landowner and farmer. For many years he lived on one of the best truck and cotton farms in the county and was for a long while one of the largest growers of fruits and vegetables in this territory. His home, located on the Humboldt-Gibson Wells road is one of the most modern in his neighborhood. Besides being a grower of truck crops he was a large producer of cotton and cattle.

Banks had been in ill health for eight months. He was active in his church, the Morning Star Baptist congregation, and was a trustee in this, Humboldt largest and newest colored religious organization.

Surviving are his wife, Zoda Banks, three daughters, Mary Sleigh of Clarksville, Tenn., Pearl Elliot of Trenton and Beatrice Cole of Humboldt. Two grandsons, Robt. Banks Cole of Humboldt and Robert Cole of the U. S. Army also survive. He also has one brother, Ollie Banks of Mountain Home, Tenn..

Funeral services were held at the Morning Star Baptist Church with the pastor, Rev. J. T. Freeman, conducting the services.

Burial followed in Motley cemetery, Humboldt.

My Grandfather Rob. B. Banks Remembered

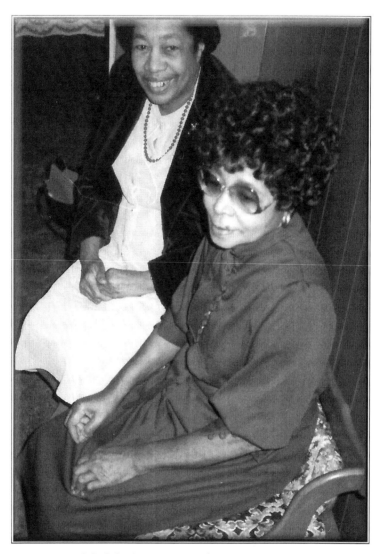

My Mother and My Aunt Pearl Elliot

Class Roll

BEATRICE MARIE BANKS
WILLIAM FRANKLIN DAVIS
ARDELLA MABEL LACY
DIMPLE LEE LAWRENCE
MILDRED VELMA LEWIS
FRANCES NELDA McLIN
MATTIE LUCILE MALONE
GENEVA ESTELLE NESBIT
MARY JANE NEWHOUSE
MARSHALL NEIL WHITE

MOTTO—Let Life Lead
COLORS—Orange and Blue
FLOWER—American Beauty Rose

1927

The Senior Class

of the

Humboldt City High School

requests the honor of your presence

at the

Commencement Exercises

Friday evening April twenty-ninth

Nineteen hundred twenty-seven

at seven o'clock

C. M. E. Church

My Mother's Graduation Program

Robert W. Cole   79

My Mother at Rest

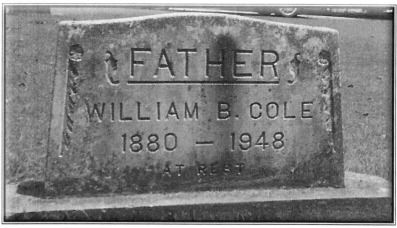

My Father at Rest

My Surrogate Mother - Ella B. Couch at age 105

TENNESSEE A & I STATE COLLEGE
Department of Music

Presents

Robert W Cole

In

Organ Recital

May 6, 1951, 7:00 p. m.

Program

Prelude And Fugue, In G Major	Bach
Sonata in C Minor	Mendelssohn

    Grave
    Adagio
    Allegro Maestoso vivace
    Fugue

A lovely Rose is Blooming	Brahms
"O Holy City, Seen of John"	Bingham
Communion	Purvis
Marche Triomphale	Dubois

My Graduation Organ Recital Program

In peace, I will lie down and
sleep; for Thou alone, O Lord, makest
me dwell in safety.   Psalm 4:8

NEW LIFE LUTHERAN CHURCH
Thurman and Norris Streets
Camden, New Jersey   08104

May 24, 1984   1:00 p.m.

PRAYER OF FAITH

God is my help in every need.
He does my every hunger feed.
He walks beside me, guides my way,
Through every moment of the day.

I now am wise, I now am true;
Patient, kind and loving too.
All things I am, can do, and be--
Through Christ, the truth that is in me.

God is my health, I can't be sick.
He is my strength, unfailing, quick.
He is my all--I'll know no fear,
For God, and love, and truth are here.

Pall Bearers

Fred L. Bennett, Jr.
Stephen W. Bryant
Harold R. Yates, Jr.
Steven C. Willoughby
Milton T. Fox
Robert Lindsey
Frank Lindsey
Glenn D. Johnson

Organists

Ms. Claudia Young
Mr. Robert Cole

The family wishes to express special
thanks to all those who have been a
source of strength and comfort during
their time of sorrow. We will be receiving
at 1264 Decatur Street, Camden, New
Jersey

My First Piano Teacher's funeral program

Robert W. Cole   *83*

In Japan

With Friedelind Wagner at the Metropolitan Opera

Conducting Spring Concert in Lawrenceville

My Son - Lamin Darboe

With Mother Divine at Spring Concert in Lawrenceville

Dear Mr. Cole,
    Having learned of your retirement, I
want to express appreciation for the cultur
literacy, music, wisdom and humanism that y
imparted to this pupil and to others in you
classroom some two decades ago. (You might
be pleased to know that I've gone on to
become associated with projects at a major
performing arts company and a stage and
television production memorializing one-hal
of a famous composer-lyricist team.) As my
other remembrances of Lawrence schools
largely fall short of those of your class,
I'll remain annonymous but thank you
sincerely for your dedication. I wish you
the very best in all your future endeavors.

My Student's Appreciation

Grand Marshal of the Strawberry Festival 2010

≈ No Regrets ≈

A Collection of Poetry

by Robert W. Cole

God is in charge

The choice is ours.

Life goes on.

There are changes to be made.

Status quo is not a go.

It is not part of being alive.

Keep living!

I told you so.

PEOPLE COME INTO YOUR LIFE,

People go out of your life.

You know I'm told

    it serves a purpose

    within a mold

    that I thought was safe.

Yet, life is real and secure

    depending on a deal.

So, move on over

    and let them go.

Get a new deal on life to know

    when to let people go.

That will be the time to relax.

When so called "friends" get the axe

    expiration date does not come late.

Forever noticed,

Purpose serviced and disconnected.

A YEAR OLDER,

A year wiser,

   A year of less talk,

A year of more learning.

A year to figure out

   who am I?

A year to find out

   where am I going?

Time, Time, Time.

   Oh, so precious.

Look all around,

   what do you see?

Was it life to be?

The error was played

   for all to see.

Lord, I must agree, the time has come

   for Thee.

Preparing to die

   by living.

Dying is a part of living.

Live your life.

Have no regrets.

Treating everyone

with respect.

Kindness a better bet yet!

No regrets.

Aging is a Witch,

an iffy prognosis.

The body machine

breaks down.

Some earlier,

some later.

The machine

needs work:

high-end maintenance.

Inherited gene.

It is the scene.

"Don't know about

life going up,

It's mighty sweet coming down."

Yes, before I go,

my intent – creating money.

Fulfilled, you said so.

Can't take

it to the grave,

you know.

≈

YOU DREAM, SO IT SEEMS.

The new broom sweeps

   clean.

The old one

   gets the dirt.

Yes, the body must get to work.

YOU KNOW IT

will end.

Time will tell.

Turn to religion

for another toll.

That will be good

for the soul.

Young and old,

Same story told.

Month or year,

Day or night,

Hopefully you will

see the light.

Then let go

without a fight.

≈

YOUR SECOND CHANCE:

No, you say,

Not today.

Let it go

    sometime.

Most of the time

    you don't get a second chance.

No "pity party,"

No "sympathy club,"

Just let it go.

Remember, I told you so.

On with it!

Yes, I must provide

    the future prison population.

≈

I'm not old,

I have just been here

   a long time,

So the story goes.

A few more years

   is my stay.

Cut the chatter,

Years don't matter.

Unless you are producing,

Still breathing – another

"Fact test."

Get over the knack.

Believe the fact.

Keep breathing.

Complete the act!

≈

"WHEN YOU HURRY

  through life

  you get to the end faster."

That causes deception

  and distress at its best.

It's not left to me

  to determine what will be.

A trust in God, you must agree.

The pain is plain for you and me.

Convert that pain for all to see.

Overcome!

Then trust, you must!

Otherwise

  you are left in the dust.

Tricky stuff.

                ≈

You are only a breath

between life and death.
Learn from others
   is my bet.
Got it!
Not yet.
Listening is an act of love.
Take a breath!
Hole in your soul?
Fill it with a word from God.
There are always two sides.
Whom do you blame?
Fix you own problem!

I don't tell grown folks

what to do

unless I'm asked.

That makes for another task.

Imposing my will

is not a thrill.

Your "down-time"

is not to give.

Just say NO

and do it SO.

Your life will reward

the keeper

And not

the reaper.

Stay in your lane

and get to the end.
It is not a sin,
  head held high with a grin.
Changes must be made,
  lest you become staid.
Adjust is a must.
The run is on us.
Can't you feel that thrust,
  whom do you trust?
Night and day, the finish
  is not in sight.
Keeper of the watch
  close at hand.
Ain't life a sham?
  Oops!
Wrong lane again.

≈

THE SUN BEGINS TO RISE,

I open my eyes to the skies.

My work begins without cries.

What must I do?

Thank God for allowing me to

    see the skies.

Things to do

    to see me through.

My day has begun,

    there is work to be done.

I can't surface without the sun.

My rise today is for the asking.

Be kind to all

    is my call.

I hope all

    see the sun rise today.

I woke up

   in my "right mind,"
No signs of decline.
That told me
   things are fine.
Just you watch.
My mind
   not left behind.
Status quo
   "Gotta go!"
Morning – Noon – Night
   What a delight!
My mind?
   "Out of sight!"

≈

I DON'T KNOW ABOUT

    tomorrow.

Today is passing

    through.

I must find something

    to do.

What time is it?

Don't blame me,

    I'm no misfit.

"Good morning"

    or

Is it afternoon?

Night will come,

Day will come,

    Repetition.

Will I make

    the transition?

    ≈

TODAY IS MINE.

Tomorrow may not come.

I may not see the rising

   of the sun

And when it comes,

My work will all be done.

Today is mine.

Tomorrow may not come.

≈

ARE YOU HEALED?

When I am old
  and gray
Please don't depart
  from me.
We all have gifts
  to help each other.
Listen – Learn – Discern.
Care comes from
  Concern.

≈

Die young

   or

Get old.

Part of the journey,

   I'm told,

is to be aware.

Do you declare?

Abuse one another?

   No!

Expect everything?

   No!

Examine the present.

Look to the future with

   hope in your heart.

Less is best.

That is the game.

The train is moving.

I must get going.

Can't you see

    what this life will be?

Stop and listen.

Will we make it?

Just wait and see

    what this life is to be.

The family has moved

into the cemetery.

The plot is filled

and not for the kill.

"Sure enough" it is real,

No big deal.

I tell you, sir

"Self for self,

and God for us all."

Judgmental is not the call.

So, it's about filled.

Does it give you

a big thrill?

The move will come

followed by the years.

Fight back the tears

and live.

≈

"WHEN SOMEONE LEAVES YOUR LIFE,

God sends someone to

   replace them."

It's not saying goodbye,

Just adding another to the supply.

   Why?

"Friends come and friends go."

Another fact, you know.

It seems to happen at every turn.

Another replacement I'd say:

   SO!

Live your life above the fray.

Yes, tomorrow is

   another day.

PEOPLE, PEOPLE EVERYWHERE.

No need to worry.

    Yes, I care.

Living this life

    will get you there.

Chances we take,

Choices we make,

Bringing life up to date.

For God's sake,

    it is in the take.

So people out there

Remake, reshape.

Life is worth living

    if you partake.

The world is not my only goal.

The spirit of life must be told.

Being of the Lord

    I have spoken.

≈

Nothing gets old

but your clothes.
That's what I'm told.
Keep moving and going,
That keeps your brain
   from slowing.
This will produce a deuce,
Strike a truce.
Never allow yourself
   to grow old.

LIFE IS LIKE

a song.

We sing it today,

Tomorrow, a delay.

What can I say?

We miss you!

There is no other way -

sad song.

The day!

Sing no more,

no delay.

Put the song away.

≈

DEAR JOHN:

Woe to me.

Don't you see

   life is yet to be?

The day has twelve hours.

What about the night?

   Twelve too?

Plenty to do,

   work on through,

   sleep on through.

What is your calling?

   Think!

Haven't you figured it out yet?

   Think!

Life is more than a bet.

≈

Total confusion

until the day you die.

I tell you

what you must do.

Find your peace

up in the sky.

Life is here and

all around you,

But for me, peace

is not found.

I'm still searching

Seeking my ground.

We think we believe

It's not what it should be.

What am I looking for?

I don't know!

Can you help me?

≈

IT'S IN THE CARDS,

It's in the choices.

You must see

 what life will be.

Getting it right

 the first time around.

Don't you see, it's up to you

 what life will be found?

Pre-empt!

Old age will not exempt the fate.

Reprisal!

Contemptuous!

What has life given thee?

  ≈

WHAT FRIENDS MEAN TO ME,

watch and see.

Stay in the moment.

Don't you know

the longer you know people

you will find them out?

Govern yourself accordingly

and do not be led in doubt.

Learn from the mistakes.

That's what it takes

to find out what life is about.

Why become a casualty

when you need not be?

Between you and me,

that's between friends.

≈

SOME COME INTO OUR LIVES

and quickly go.

Some people become

friends

And stay awhile,

Leaving beautiful footprints

on our hearts.

And we are never quite the same

because we have made a good friend.

≈

MY HAND HURTS,

My fingers ache.

Lord knows, I'm not sad.

At my age, you know!

Get up early,

   can't sleep, you know.

I'm trying not to weep

At my age, you know!

Start my day

   with my bath.

Paper at the door.

Vinegar and honey,

   that's a must.

That's the remedy I've

    learned to trust.

At my age, you know!

Some breakfast too,

   a light one, you know.

Just something

   to make me go.

At my age, you know!

I'm holding on

    and moving.

The phone is gonna ring:

    my son, you know.

Others, too

    will call to say

"Anything I can do for you today?"

"No darling!"

My hand is hurting,

    but "I'm doing fine."

"Keep in touch."

"I'll be on the line."

≈

WHO AM I?

I breathe.

My heart beats.

I don't need a "tweet."

Life is real – "Neat."

What am I to do?

We are not severed from life

   yet!

Connect to life.

We have a choice.

Life takes its turn.

It's all about choices.

"Ghetto" – Maybe!

"Priorities" – Yes!

It's Monday,

   a new day,

   a new week.

Start all over

   without defeat.

It is ours to keep.

Wake up!

Can't you do with less sleep?

Don't worry about what

　　you can do to get you through.

Less negativity is my clue.

Be more positive is our

　　wake up call

　　that should be for all.

Change the mind of people,

　　you must!

Life can be complete

Think!

It's Monday again

Rethink!

Will you get through?

It's Monday!

Why be blue?

Within me my happiness lies.

　　≈

GIVE YOUR BRAIN A REST,

that should be an easy test.
Today's world you must
multi-task:
Radio blasting.
Ear phone blasting.
Tweeting and texting.
As we go
no rest no less.
Delete if we must,
just another step.
My brain says "Help!"
On the go, ready or not.
"Just leave me be."
Maybe, I'll find time
for recovery.

≈

CELEBRITIES

want to be seen.

Recognize me?

What do you see?

Is it a tree?

Is it a stump?

I am higher than that stump.

I could jump.

Can't you see me?

My spirit is keen.

Free yourself.

Let it go.

Trouble gone – out the do'.

Don't celebrate the fate.

Elevate yourself.

Oops!

Start over.

≈

TITLES MEAN NOTHING

when the job is over.

So where do we go?

Was it all for show?

You said it!

I have my title and no place

to go.

You guessed it!

It was all for show.

No more.

Out the door!

Away from me!

You know

I have grown.

What about you?

Some old ways

to see you through.

Exposure!

Have mercy on you.

That same "old web"

    caught you, I know.

Just can't let go.

Exposure!

Off you go.

It's a must!

Exposure!

    ≈

IT'S YOUR TURN

Don't you ever learn?

Yes, it's your turn

Deal with it!

Don't throw cautions
   to the wind.

It will lead you
   to the end.

Yet, life will help you win.

That's no sin.

It follows every generation.

We are wonderfully blessed.

Forget about the rest.

That is the best.

≈

THE ANCHOR IS SMALL.

You stand tall.

Birthday or not,

    that's what Allah wrought.

Sea or land,

A ship with sails,

    runs its course.

Day in – day out.

Birthdays sought,

    no doubt.

Blessings restored,

    son and wife adored.

Birthday wishes:

    "All Aboard!"

≈

love and gone.

Carver days

good days shown.

Carver days

bad days blown.

You can't have it all

without tone.

Yes, true to the bugle call.

But the students

were standing tall.

1-2-3-4

Orange – Rappahannock

Madison – Culpepper.

We welcome thee.

All getting an education.

Yes, we welcome thee.

Don't you see, our life was

yet to be?

Yes – yes!

Carver you and me.

Some are gone,

   crossed over, you see.

Some are here.

Ours, yet another day.

Life is giving.

Don't you see?

Carver – "Forever"

For you and me.

MIGHTY GRAND,

Mighty bold,

Restless and cold.

Young, you know!

The story told,

    shaped to fit the mold.

"You can't send the baby back."

Out on your own,

    let it be known

    you are not alone.

Seeds have seen sown.

The baby shown.

Instantly grown,

"Don't you wish"

    this to be known?"

Diapers too.

What am I to do?

"You can't send the baby back."

Do you lack the knack?

Why back-track?

"You can't send the baby back."

≈

THEY WAIT

> and

You are not there.

That's a new meaning to declare.

You will be missed.

We do know that.

Trinity –FATHER, SON, AND HOLY GHOST.

LORD, "Bless us all before we go."

Yes, we hope to meet

> some day, you know.

Life goes on

> without our own.

That is shown.

Memories are there

> to declare.

Rest your SOUL

> and love is still,

> that is the deal.

Life will continue,

It's GOD's will.

Blessings and Mercy are our plight.

Living and dying are our call.

Blessings and Mercy

will be shared by All.

YOU HAVE BEEN THROUGH

worse storms than this.

Trust in God.

You will find bliss.

No need to worry.

I tell you this:

God is there.

Fret no more.

Be on the go.

Leave your troubles

at the door.

The storm has passed

to another shore.

≈

Find the Holy

    Spirit in everyone.

Spirit un-ending,

    in the light,

      guides us to where we must go,

      to the color and the show.

That's Feeling, you know.

Darkness weaves a negative sight.

It is without the light.

Be done –

    just wait 'til morn'.

        ≈

Blame God.

Are you sure?

Friends and foe

add to the test.

A mess is just a mess.

Just confess!

No wisdom there,

I guess.

Old and wise

is just a disguise.

Feelings and hurt are here.

Is that clear?

Another day is near

How do you respond?

With love and compassion?

No, I don't complain.

What is there to gain?

Negativity is on the wane.

Love and kindness

    are my tick.

The power comes from God,

    not the lightning rod.

In a clear voice, I got the call:

Stand tall,

"You heard it all."

Is God part of the plan?

We find God in ourselves.

What do you hear?

What do you see?

There is no love like His.

Is God part of the plan?

Center yourself in the
    Spirit of God.

With heart and mind
    in photo-op.

Then receive the wisdom
    that is at hand.

Be awesome believers.

Don't you dare think
    He is not there.

Give, care and share.

Without God, my plans
    go nowhere.

≈

ONE WAY JESUS

is alright.

He's got the power

over day and night.

He has the power

over the dead

in the grave.

Jesus one way is alright.

≈

"WHEN THE WICKED WILL CEASE

    from trembling, and

    the weary be at rest."

We have floated on the

    edge of existence.

Have we given up the primal

    desire to live?

Stay with us, Lord Jesus.

Restore balance to my body and mind.

I will not sink because

    God's grace keeps me afloat.

The flow of life is seen as the tide

    comes in: FREEDOM!

The tide washes out.

We seek peace.

≈

Finding peace within

is a good way to begin.
Turn within to coexist and
find peace again.
Doubt is no way out
of our infectious thoughts.
Unkindness without reason
will lead to treason
in any season.
When peace is unconditional
and part of the picture,
my confidence is accountable.
I confide in peace.
Don't you see
what your life is to be?

≈

THE PLAYING ANGELS,

    three in number,

    who walk with me.

Three you see,

    a symbol of Trinity

    for me.

Each morning or afternoon

    is a time to see

    what life ought to be.

One can interact within life's journey

    with the Maker day to day

    in a spiritual way.

Be aware of the spark within

    as the angels light the way

    for the promise of that day.

Don't you want to see the angels?

≈

THE LORD MADE US ALL.

Let lightning and thunder

  give us a call.

The hand of God is behind it all.

The results will be what they will be.

What did I do?

  I have done no wrong,

That is my song.

  Why punish me?

Just let me be.

  What did I do?

Answer me.

Free my spirit

  so I can live.

≈

"THINGS WILL RIGHT

themselves."

Just don't do something wrong.

Promises made in overtime:

Temptations.

Stand there!

Choices we make will be there

to take.

The price is not a fake.

Life's lessons will find you out.

All truths don't have to be known.

Watch and pray,

just you wait for another day

of Divine Intervention.

See, I told you so.

Wrong has to go.

Watch and pray,

just you wait for another day.

I told you so.

≈

I BOW MY HEAD

and say a prayer.
Pray and do what you
have to do.
It is God who will see
you through.
You must be exposed
if you are to be satisfied.
It's never too late
to fill this date.
We pray and just wait.
There is no time or date,
just you wait!
Don't be anxious.
Ain't life great!

≈

ISAIAH WAS THE OTHER PROPHET,

A life filled for all to see.

A human being and what is to be,

    kindness and decency to a "T."

That's my Isaiah, you see.

History will tell the story.

For all to see; don't you agree?

My Isaiah, Rebecca and thee.

Time spent well

    is not a hard sell.

We have work to do.

Let's not forget.

It's for you too

    with no regrets.

GOOD BYE, GOD.

I have been to college.

It is to know

   all there is to know.

A show for sure

   that I must endure.

To let you think

   I am secure.

Another day we meet head on

   thinking that life is a song.

Doing your best and seeing it

   go wrong.

Yes, I've been to college.

   The song is gone.

≈

THERE ARE RISKS

associated with life.

Look to God for release.

Some say in life

"Where do we find peace?"

"Will life give us some release?"

The questions are yours and mine.

Don't you agree?

For life might set us free.

That is up to you and me.

≈

LOOK IN THE MIRROR AND

   see one's self.

Start healing.

Read the Bible.

God speaks to me.

God is speaking about me.

The face is the show.

The soul is to go.

Lord, what do I know?

≈

IT'S ALL ABOUT THE BIBLE,

you see.

Mrs. "B" told you so.

That should be enough to agree.

We study on Wednesday, you see.

Hold on, don't let it go.

There's more to come

from the "sixty-six," you know.

Teach us well.

I don't hear the bell.

Mrs. "W" expounding and pounding.

Acknowledge it! Let it go!

Why confuse Ms. "D"?

You don't need tricks or any hard licks.

Re-calculate.

The teacher explains it.

Why don't you get it?

Sleep on Ms. "E," your life is a snooze.

Yes, we do understand:

    the BIBLE is our plan,

    a way of life is at hand.

It's Wednesday, you see.

Yes, it's for us to know

    there's birthday wishes from this clan.

To divide or not to divide?

We must integrate
   and fight for the right.
That fight is out of sight.
Is that a delight?
I am part of
   "The Main Stream."
Found your identity?
That must be part of
   the dream.
Out of this
   I do my own thing.
Now that this is done
   the rules are forgotten.
We want our own.
Have we truly grown?
Why segregate?
The facts are not known.
   Does it matter?

As long as we move

   With "our own."

We need to

   Integrate

Before we

   Disintegrate.

≈

INTEGRATION OR NOT,

the journey is hard.

Win or lose,

is that smart?

It will be with us

from the start.

Standards?

Yes, we do depart

Separate?

We do get smart.

Ways and means?

we know how to treat that part.

Remove the clutter

without a shudder.

We have departed

from smartness.

To the other,

"Mercy be, my brother"

Can't we see how to get

out of the gutter?

In spite of circumstances

I will survive.

That is,

if I find the rudder.

≈

WITH MY MIGHT,

    do I find delight in the fight?

It was 1965 Civil Rights.

Johnson was there in sight.

Every day is not Sunday.

Distractions galore.

Man, I can't find the door.

Schools fall apart.

You owe me some more.

Reparations – about to start.

"Crabs in a barrel."

Thou art caught

What do you see pulling after me?

Speak or keep moving.

Go to jail or "rehab."

Rehabilitate another way,

    so they say.

All die along the way.

See you when there is a

    better day.

≈

Some people

   yes, my people

   spend a life creating anxiety.

Where do we go from here?

It is up to me or is it thee?

Can't you see the conflict in me?

Thank God! I don't deal with this every day.

Makes me crazy like a daisy.

Do I need to hear it?

I can't fix it.

Just let it be.

Will you ever see

   the need to be free?

Things are not what they could be,

   they are what they are.

Bless the Being from afar.

ANOTHER CULTURE

you have created:
Whites – Blacks
Brown – Tattooed
Another class,
where do we go?
Free food,
More drama,
More chaos,
No morality,
Project mentality,
Object to learning,
Object to education,
"Yes, I does"
You know what I mean,
Told you so,
Let it go.
Wait! Wait! Entertainment!
Yes, yes.

Watch the show.

Reality is here to stay.

Don't forget

I told you so.

≈

SHAKE THE DUST OFF.

Stay white,

    the other man

    without the tan.

Just bland

    in the land.

Wave to the crowd.

Make me good.

Someday I will be understood.

≈

WHAT CAN I GET

for nothing?

Time to explore - you bet -

like it or not.

My mind tells me

what I've got.

Is it a lot?

Is it a long shot?

Get it going.

Redeem your winnings.

Lessen the blow.

"One for the money,

"One for the show."

Stupidity!

Is that the way to go?

LIFE IS NOT ALWAYS FAIR.

Is there something you
    must declare?
Life isn't always fair.
Work hard, dedicate
    yourself to something.
It still could be taken
    from you.
Trust and faith,
    they are a must.
You must adjust.
Yes, that's life.
Another bet, does it
    leave you in debt?
You will see,
    you must agree,
    life is full of mystery.

≈

LIFE IS A STRUGGLE.

No "rose garden" here.

Get up each day,

   do what you must.

Plan and design your day,

   get away from the fray.

What do you say?

Excitement is not for me,

   no drama, you see.

"Every truth don't have

   to be told."

Even if you are old,

   you see the world as you grow,

   filter and all.

The view is clear: what makes you

   think I will change?

Why be defensive?

What do we replace it with?

Dysfunction is key.

≈

DON'T YOU SEE?

Destruction will yet be.

What do we replace it with?

Who am I?

Open up.

Dismiss the crowd.

Part of the church

  being saved.

You are in.

Where do you begin?

See and feel the world.

≈

Hypocrisy is alive

and well.

Live and tell the stories well.

Grins and fakes are part of the game.

One for the wake, another for the take.

Too much time on your hands.

Manufactured problems do dwell.

Live and learn how to express your concern.

Don't be caught in the web.

Lord, have mercy.

I will never tell.

WHEN WILL THE

   bubble burst?

Who can you trust?

First and last – a must.

So, why pretend?

Life goes on

   and yet

   somehow I must defend and

   pretend!

Back where I started.

Grin and pretend.

≈

TALENT VERSUS PERSONALITY.

Isn't that a reality?

Arrogance and ego

   have got to go.

Need to ask for more.

Imitation is about to cover.

Development is less.

Annoyance is at its best.

Life of a fake and

   fluff is no test.

Move on, let it go.

Accept it or not.

Neglected!

Schizophrenic is the name.

Whom do I blame?

I AM GOING TO DO

something the

Devil won't do.

I am going to take leave

from you.

Don't you know

that's what I do?

Yes, it's true.

Devil and me

caught in the melee.

To and fro – up and around.

Man alive, I can't be bound.

Life's lessons must be sound.

I'll just say "good-bye" for now.

≈

REAPING DAY IS COMING.

Sow bad seeds and

   you will reap what you sow.

Letting you know

   before you go.

You will reap what you sow

   day in and day out.

Repent the event

   bad or good, yet understood.

Deeds done wrong,

Fields of clutter,

Dare to utter

   "You will reap what you sow."

≈

You can't live

crooked and

die straight.

Why not choose

another gait?

Life is there

for all to be

the best you can be.

Don't you see?

Well, the rest

is up to me.

≈

Inner peace is

mine to care.

Inner peace is

mine to share.

Trust me! Just you dare.

Outer faking is a bust.

Caring about life is a must.

It is my motto.

Yes, believe and trust.

Peaceful living

without fuss.

≈

"A HEAP SEES,

    but a few knows."

Granny gave me words to grow

    on life's journey.

Why grow old with it not told?

Yesterday's news is today's headlines.

Can't you see?

The famous

    giving out quotes by rote.

Forget the note.

Why enter into their lifestyles?

Let it go.

Trust God.

"Life goes on."

That is the song.

Can you see where it belongs?

≈

Long may you live,

    long may you tarry.

Kiss whom you please,

    but mind whom you marry.

Watch what people do

    and not what they say.

My oh my! That's the better way.

"Learn to listen"

    that's what I say.

That is the way.

    Just say "nay" or

    is it "yay"?

      ≈

THE LONGER YOU LIVE

you learn how to live.

Give and listen,

mind what you do.

Is there a better way?

Excuse the verse.

My, it's terse.

Do you need to be

in control of everything?

≈

Sense of entitlement

makes a difference.

Don't succumb

or even play dumb.

Time will tell, you know,

very well.

Why fall for that spell?

Can't you tell

that it doesn't sit well?

Let it go.

I told you so.

Emit!

No more!

≈

"BE TOO BIG

    to be little"

    the saying goes.

For all to hear,

    let the words be clear

    yet another year.

"Don't look behind the door."

I told you so.

My destination is

    how to survive.

≈

Cantankerous people

   must change themselves.

It's a want

   not for me.

It's for you.

The will of God

   for you to work through.

Why be a nuisance?

Is it option one or option two?

Immature and obnoxious

   is my beat.

You find that indiscreet?

Instant message – sarcastic – cumbersome.

Yet! Cumbersome to the core and more!

Sarcasm is my defense.

Do I need pretense?

WORDS, WORDS, WORDS.

Meaningless words.

Condemn yourself

    by what you say.

Why wait another day?

Take a bit of air.

Open your mouth – let it out.

No need to shout.

Help me to overcome

    that doubt.

For Thy will be done.

Yes, there is hope.

≈

LONELY PEOPLE ARE MEDDLESOME.

Lonely people are troublesome.

Are you confused or just used?

Trouble is the game.

Everyone shows some blame.

Is it too late to change?

Stay in line

   out of my space.

Mind your place.

That's my take on a fake.

Slow down.

Don't be meddlesome.

What's the use?

It makes life a deuce.

Where is the ace?

≈

DON'T BE A NUISANCE.

Floating around,
    feet off the ground
    with nothing to do.
Making talk
    just for flair.

≈

FOR GOD'S SAKE!

Come up for air.

It's a dare, I do declare

    for you to see.

I hope you get it.

It is plain for me to see.

Do you agree; can't you see?

Keep your mouth closed

    before you become disposed.

SHUT UP!

≈

Too much information.

Can't you save something

    for next Sunday?

Apologize!

Enough is too much.

Too much has to be enough.

Straightforwardness!

Speak of truth,

    falsehood and lies.

From these lips in disguise

    what is it you need to hear?

Help us in our time of need.

Too much greed.

People are watching us.

Can we find respect, obedience,

    and kindness?

You know how inadequate I am,

    less haughtiness you see.

Let me go! I need contentment.

What is it to you?

Why do I need to know that
   ungrateful response?

Behaving badly.

GOSSIP BY

Cable or phone.

Are you prone?

Talking anonymously.

You are prone?

Petits fours or sweets,

    you don't need a treat.

"Mind your business"

    is my tweet.

The scenario is replaying.

What good does it do you?

What is it to you?

Tune it out.

Gossip dubbed – no doubt.

Version dead – doubt what's said.

I'm still talking.

Crucial – For what?

Critical enthusiasm – objective.

Mouth diarrhea malfunctioning.

≈

IT'S THE RIGHT THING TO DO.

Lord, I can't help it.

You will see me through

    because You know

    that is what You do.

Sometimes up and sometimes down,

    you know I'll keep my feet on the ground.

Freedom is my goal, yes, I have been told.

Hate leads to debate – why retaliate?

Face the future without fear,

    presuming happiness is near.

Do I need to understand?

It's the right thing to do.

Stop and pause – let it catch up with you.

Give thanks and confess.

It's the right thing to do.

Just keep on being.

No stress!

    ≈

Robert W. Cole   *191*

STEP AWAY FROM BUSINESS,

your time will expand.
Slow down and live with
less stress!
Your body needs a rest.
Why take it to a test?
Reconnect!
Where are you going?
What are you doing?
I simply need to be
just me.
Shake the dust,
let it roll on.
That which is to be
always is.

THE LOUDEST SILENCE

I have heard.

Where are you going?

What are you doing?

Time will tell.

Will you go on pursuing,

 aiming for naught?

Come on, entertain a thought.

See what the world has wrought.

Your life need not be for naught.

The power of the pause:

 be yourself

 not surrounded by noise.

Is that a better cause?

Be blessed.

≈

What have I done?

Where are you going?

The time will come.

The work is not done.

What will I do?

Is it too late to

    see it through?

No one told me

    what I must do.

Yet, I know it all.

Why not divert the call?

Lord, it's too late

    for me to abdicate

What do I do?

Disintegrate!

≈

COMMITMENT AND YOU ARE

about to be through.

Courageous or not,

animation is sought.

Resentment and contention

is our expectancy.

Confrontation will recriminate.

Just you wait!

Negative conniving

is our "who dunnit?."

Speculative "faux pas"

is draining,

Suspicious pretending

per se

is not my way.

≈

COMMITMENTS COME,

Commitments go.

Cajole, manipulate

   both are seen

   at the door.

Keeping your commitments

   is a must.

Sum it up to dust.

Do it or bust.

Shake the curse,

   self-reinvent is my take.

Pure folly, take my warning,

   why become a fake?

Learn from your mistakes.

That's what Mama

   taught.

Look at what you did.

That's what Mama

   thought.

Was it for naught?

You didn't get caught!

It's just a thought.

Mistakes made? Yes!

Confess to the mess? No!

Something's gotta go,

   mistake or me.

Wait and see

   before Mama

   sets me free.

≈

I AM GOING TO

do it

and

I am going to do it well.

Time will tell,

how swell!

I did it, you bet, you tell.

Inspiration versus perspiration.

It was my goal.

The rest is to be told

Get going! Never dispel.

That's not a rough sell.

Knowledge, of course,

with creativity in tow

biblically attached.

We found a match

Latched.

It's your call.

We did it well.

≈

I MARCHED FOR THIS!

Apologizing defeats the threat.

Education destroyed the cause.

On the bottom of life

   it does matter.

No applause.

Life on the bottom,

   not a sight in view.

What are we to do?

Life on the bottom

   day to day.

Opt for another way.

≈

ONE GENERATION GOES,

Another generation comes.

Compare – Prepare.

I declare – 'tis so.

Do you need to know any more?

Right!

Get yourself up,

   you must agree.

Don't you see?

Generations come and go.

"The climb is easy,

   the fall is hard."

Is that your call?

≈

Sub-culture ventriloquist

Show me limitations – **No!**

My self-image left at the door.

I'll substitute it for sure.

Let me out of here.

I'll be flippant no more.

Overwhelming to that score.

"I feel like a failure!"

Hype – walking or riding,

Patronizing – running or sprinting,

Suspicious – frayed and traditional.

Reward the good and punish the bad.

Oh how sad to be not understood.

Manipulate every situation.

Bad words make good news.

Too much ego – can't let it go.

The mix is there.

I don't care – is that a dare?

Indignant to the cause,

    hypocrisy is my bent.

Phony must be at the end.

That will be my claim because

    you are better than no one,

    but you can be everyone's equal.

Speculation and rumor is the source.

Whom do you trust?

Humans are made for each other.

Before it's too late,

    control you space.

Manipulate!

Money now is

    the name of the game.

Shame on you if you have nothing to blame.

Just got caught or was I bought?

Can't explain – what a mess wrought.

Sight, hearing, taste, touch and smell,

    the five senses that make us tell.

We do things that don't sit well.

However, it's done and

    I don't know why.

Just another day and a weak alibi.

I must try, never say die,

    find my senses in the sky.

GOING OUT?

Out into the world?

My cause would be

    natural you see

    not because of stupidity.

Life is not easy

    or convenient.

Multiply by three

    to see what I see.

Why disconnect?

Participate in the notion.

Smart one

    1 2 3

Intelligence!

What will it be?

    1 2 3

Races of people,

    what will it be?

1 2 3

Don't you see?

What's in it for me?

Instant existence.

1 2 3

≈

Reduce everything

to accommodate the masses.

Listen, think for yourself.

It's all about me:

Cheat – Beat – Deceit.

Find it not in defeat.

It is not neat.

Consider it conceit.

You must retreat.

We are made for

each other.

The control has got

to go.

Your space lives here

no more.

≈

I'M READY FOR THE RIDE,

    changing with the fads and the tides.

"Déjà vu" all over again.

The train is leaving – I must hurry.

Can't be left.

My disguise is ready for fooling

    even with some schooling.

The scenario remains the same:

    Who am I fooling?

      ≈

DON'T BREAK THE BUBBLE.

That means trouble.

Thankful or not,

    self-image is the plot.

Survive or not,

    I will get caught.

Fantasy wrought

    without ability working.

What's my pledge?

I live

    on the edge.

≈

DON'T LET ANYONE USE YOU.

I told you so.

Now what do you do?

It's part of your talk:

   Get it!

Learn it before you walk

   then you see what life is meant to be.

Use me or not.

I see through your plot.

Best take another shot.

Trickster or not,

   you must be from some Lot.

Amazing! Use me!

I get it.

Personal agenda – dot.

Revealing:

   Am I a user?

     ≈

DON'T ALLOW YOURSELF

to be used.

Stop it!

Reject the muse.

Why be used?

Is that what you choose?

Alignment is clear.

You do understand, dear,

loud and clear,

nothing to fear.

Don't let others use you.

Things you do,

Things you did not do,

What a mess!

Fail the test?

Use me, I guess.

What a fool!

Figure it out.

Delete the rest.

≈

DON'T GO DOWN

   to "Funk Land."

It is too crowded.

Get up!

Get going!

Prepare yourself

   for the showing.

There is no need for

   destroying.

Get up!

Get going!

Why be negative?

Rejuvenated!

Get going!

What God has planned

   is in His hands.

"Geezus!"

    ≈

What's the use?

Project mentality

   from the streets,

   you know,

   that mentality must go.

Leave it alone

   with a frown or a groan.

Yes, street mentality,

   all of its own,

   the ugliness must be shown.

≈

H<small>E MIGHT BE MY</small>

   C<small>OLOR</small>

but he ain't my

   K<small>IND</small>!

Letting you know

   I ain't blind.

Build or kill,

    which is the will?

Just sit still.

Another dreamer

   to attract.

It's just a fact.

History will help

   as we look back

   in fact!

    ≈

THIS DISCLOSURE BRINGS DEEP REMORSE,

sad exposure.

Change yourself,

remake and take.

That looks like a fake.

You can't change anyone

but yourself.

That is a definite re-take.

For God's sake

RE-TAKE!

≈

Amplifying a life to live,

the "low-down" folks,

so-called "common element,"

will they destroy it?

Echoes of the past

do not lend

themselves to fright.

Can't you see?

You must not be wrapped tight.

Reconstruction has started.

Deconstruction tempts us

with flight.

What about your attitude?

You don't get it!

Let it go.

Try to learn some more

at least before you go.

You have been part of the

universe, you know

DON'T YOU SEE YOURSELF

through the eyes of others?
"The eyes of the master

does more work than

two hands."
Despicable!
Is that part of the curse?
Things do get worse
Show me how to reverse

the Curse.

≈

The world today

is not what it was yesterday.

Fifteen minutes of fame,

whom do you blame?

Write your book,

think you're famous

for the day

without delay.

Famous for that part of the stay:

"local loud mouth."

What do you have to say?

Nay, nay, nay.

You will delay the play.

No skills – not the way.

What do you say?

Not in my household today.

"You work for what you get."

You know the rules.

Follow the exit sign.

It was by design.

≈

FORESIGHT OR HINDSIGHT,

do you need approval?

I told you so!

There has to be

another way to go.

Should have,

Would have,

Could have.

No strategic planning

without a doubt.

Can't you find another way out?

Meetings and reports and

intentions may be good.

Take a look!

Where have you stood?

Solidify your thoughts,

find another alibi.

Negative energy

stay away!

Leave it alone.

Let it be gone.

Karma is a must.

Whom do we trust?

It is just there – a must or a bust.

Too much too soon?

It's all gone now – you bet!
Celebrity time
  before the decline.
Find another line.
Lord, what am I to do?
I'd say to you:

Finished!

≈

IT'S BOUND TO HAPPEN

sooner or later – just you wait.

What is the date?

I'll wait my fate

≈

IF YOU CANNOT AFFORD THE PUNISHMENT,

don't commit the crime.

Are you afraid of me?

Why am I a tiger?

Whatever the mind

of man can conceive

and believe, it can achieve.

It's a poor cook who's hungry,

pots and pans everywhere.

Can't you see? – hungry no more!

That's not me – Don't you agree?

≈

The "W" world

can be gruesome.

Are you Mayflower

registered?

Give a cheer for thee.

I must not disagree.

You know where to talk.

Lord have mercy.

Boring to the bone.

Indentured or not.

It's not for the talk.

Can I fix it? I will try.

Yes, 'til I die.

≈

The Baby *

MiGHTy GRAND ...   Mighty bold
"Young, you know"- "Restless and Cold
            "Young, you know"-THE STORY TOLD
                    * Shaped TO FIT the MOLD
"You can't send the baby back".

Out on your own - Let it be known
            You are Not ALONe
seeds have been soun
        THE BABY SHOWN - Instantly GROWN
"DON'TCHA Wish — this be known?"

Life will change - diapers too ...
                    WHAT AM I to do?
        "You can't send THE Baby back."
Do you lack the knack? Why back track?
" YOU CAN'T send the BABY BACK."

            Bob Cole 3·20·16   MB
                                          16

* POem DEDICATED to "BABY" DARBOE.

Holding Essah Darboe, my first grandchild born in America

≈ About the Author ≈

Robert W. Cole was born in Humboldt, Tennessee, and lived in Tennessee until graduating from Tennessee A. & I. University in Nashville, Tennessee. Wherever his curiosity and thrust for learning led him, Bob Cole always carried some of his Humboldt traditions with him: devotion to family and the firm values instilled; attachment to the church (and especially church music); and enthusiasm as clear and true as the Tennessee skies. After a brief stay in Mississippi as band director of a high school, Mr. Cole was called into the army, where he served as chaplain's assistant at the end of the Korean Conflict. On leaving this tour of duty, Mr. Cole enrolled at Ohio State University. After a year of study, he took a job teaching music in Wakeman, Ohio while studying privately at the Oberlin Conservatory of Music.

Moving to the East Coast, Mr. Cole earned a graduate degree from Penn State University and did post graduate work at Temple University while teaching in public and private schools in the Philadelphia area. Mr. Cole established strong transplanted roots in his Philadelphia neighborhood of Powelton Village where his energy, commitment and concern earned him the affectionate title of "The Mayor." He chaired a volunteer committee for The Philadelphia Orchestra and was house manager for the Walnut Street Theater, America's oldest theater. During his Philadelphia years, Mr. Cole became acquainted with the fabled African-American actor, singer and social activist, Paul Robeson. Mr. Cole retired from teaching music in Lawrenceville, New Jersey, where he excelled as an educator in the Middle School. He was also an adjunct instructor in music at the College of New Jersey in Trenton. Without the determination and prodding from many friends, none of these achievements would have been possible.

63369455R00126

Made in the USA
Charleston, SC
31 October 2016